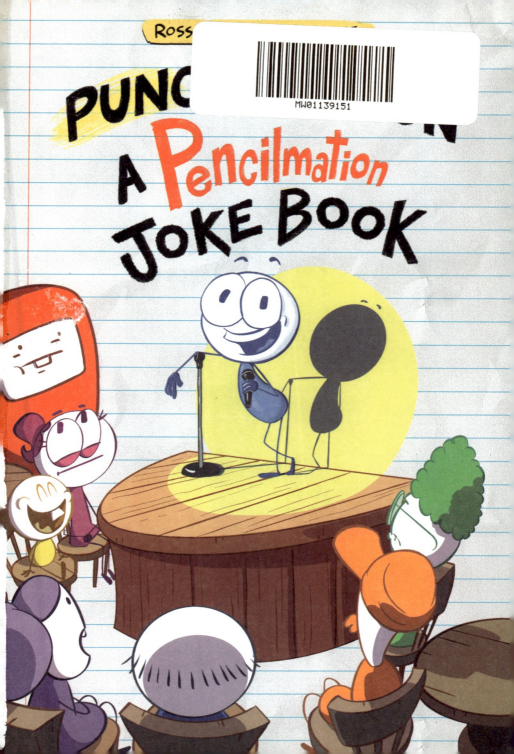

PENGUIN YOUNG READERS LICENSES
AN IMPRINT OF PENGUIN RANDOM HOUSE LLC, NEW YORK

FIRST PUBLISHED IN THE UNITED STATES OF AMERICA BY PENGUIN YOUNG READERS LICENSES,
AN IMPRINT OF PENGUIN RANDOM HOUSE LLC, NEW YORK, 2023

PHOTO CREDITS: MARKERS (8, 17, 32): LEMON_TM/ISTOCK/GETTY IMAGES; RIPPED COLORED PAPER
(5, 7, 9, 12, 13, 19, 20, 23, 25, 26, 28, 31, 32): HAPPYFOTO/ISTOCK/GETTY IMAGES

VISIT US ONLINE AT PENGUINRANDOMHOUSE.COM.

MANUFACTURED IN CHINA

ISBN 9780593522851

10 9 8 7 6 5 4 3 2 1 HH

DESIGN BY TAYLOR ABATIELL

# BY LAUGHING AT PENCILMATE, OF COURSE!

How do you greet a friend and laugh at them at the same time?

L-O-HELLO!

What do you get when you combine a dunce cap and a fairy tale?

# DUNCE UPON A TIME!

# Why did Pencilmate trip Pencilmiss on their big date?

## SO SHE WOULD FALL FOR HIM!

## Why did Pencilmate swallow a net?

### BECAUSE HE FELT LIKE HE HAD BUTTERFLIES IN HIS STOMACH!

## What do you get when you cross macaroni and cheese with a surprise kiss?

# SMACK-A-RONI AND CHEESE!

What are some of Granny's favorite recipes?

GRAN-BERRY SAUCE, GRAN-CAKES, AND GRAN-BURGERS!

KNOCK-KNOCK.

Who's there?

KISSA.

Kissa who?

KISSA YOUR FACE!

# What do you get when you cross bubble gum and Pencilmate's farts?

# BUBBLE-BUTT!

## What did Pencilmate say when he sneezed while chewing gum?

**AAAAH-CHEW!**

## What's the most dangerous type of gum?

# BUBBLE TROUBLE!

# What's Pencilmate's favorite kind of party?

# A SLURP-RISE PARTY!

**What type of snack would you find in Pencilmiss's house?**

## DRAW-BERRY SHORTCAKES!

**What type of cookies did Pencilmate bake?**

## SNICKER-DOODLES!

Why are Pencilmate's sneakers
covered in bandages?

# HE KEPT GETTING
# SPRINTERS.

Why is Pencilmate
always runner-up?

**HE'S STILL FIGURING
OUT THE *WRITE*
WAY TO RUN!**

Why does Pencilmate wear a helmet on the dance floor?

# BECAUSE HE'S AFRAID TO *BREAK* DANCE!

Why is Pencilmate always dancing at the dentist's office?

# HE JUST LEARNED HOW TO *FLOSS!*

How would Pencilmate battle a space villain?

# BY USING HIS DORK SIDE.

What is Pencilmiss's favorite button to press in a space shuttle?

# THE SPACE BAR!

Why did Pencilmate bring a frying pan to space?

# HE HEARD ABOUT ALL THE MEAT-EORS!

Did you hear about Pencilmate's road trip?

# HE FOUND A PORK IN THE ROAD!

What do you get when you meet hogs on vacation?

## PIG-PEN PALS!

What is Pencilmate's dream job?

# AN ERASE-CAR DRIVER!

Why did Pencilmate's phone keep falling asleep?

BECAUSE HE DOWNLOADED TOO MANY NAPS!

How do you know if there's a monster under your bed?

YOU CAN HEAR IT MON-STOMPING AROUND!

How do you put a cyclops to bed?

SING IT LULLAB-EYES!

What's the easiest— but slowest— way to reach Infinity Snail?

BY INFINITY MAIL!

When he's not saving Jollyville, what does Infinity Snail do in his spare time?

WATCH SAVED BY THE SHELL ON HIS SHELL-E-VISION!

How fast can Infinity Snail really go?

AS FAST AS AN ES-CAR-GO!

What do onlookers say when they see
Infinity Snail save the day?

# SNAILED IT!

How does Infinity Snail
defeat supervillains?

## BY SLUG-GING THEM,
## OF COURSE!

What is Infinity Snail's favorite brand of soda?

**GASTRO-POP!**

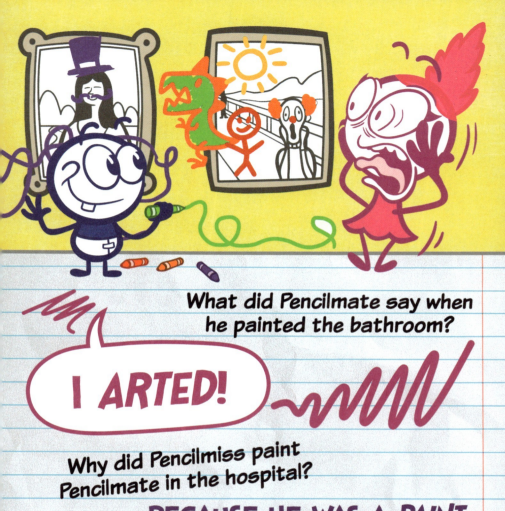

What did Pencilmate say when he painted the bathroom?

**I ARTED!**

Why did Pencilmiss paint Pencilmate in the hospital?

**BECAUSE HE WAS A PAINT IN THE NECK!**

What did the artist keep saying in jail?

**"I WAS FRAMED!"**

What is a zombie's favorite type of comedy?

# DEAD-PAN.

Why did the zombie leave his umbrella at home?

## HE WANTED IT TO *BRAAAAIN* ON HIS PARADE!

What did the zombie say at Thanksgiving?

PASS THE GRAVE-Y . . .

What is Big Guy's favorite lunch?

**A KNUCKLE SANDWICH!**

What do you get when you cross Big Guy and a car salesman?

**A BIG DEAL!**

How does Big Guy stay so strong?

**HE EATS PLENTY OF MUSCLE SPROUTS!**

What time is it when Big Guy sits on a clock?

# TIME TO GET A NEW CLOCK!

When did Granny know it was time to go to the dentist?

## BECAUSE IT WAS TOOTH-HURTY!

Why did Tall Guy put a clock on his guitar?

# SO HE COULD ROCK AROUND THE CLOCK!

What happens when you ask
Mini-Mate for the time?

HE GETS TICKED OFF!

How is Pencilmiss
like a clock?

SHE *TOCKS* WAY
TOO MUCH!

Why did Pencilmate bite the clock?

HE SAID HE WAS
HUNGRY FOR
SECONDS!

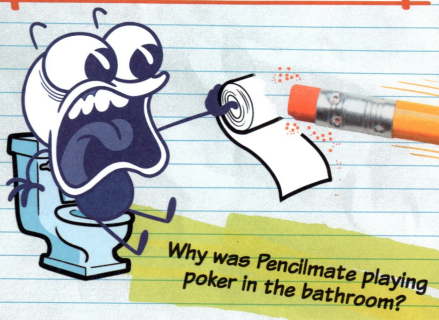

Why did Pencilmate decorate his room with periodic tables?

# THEY MADE HIM FEEL LIKE HE WAS IN HIS *ELEMENT!*

What's the best way to compliment a geologist?

TELL HER SHE *ROCKS!*

What do you get when you cross a pig and a dinosaur?

**JURASSIC PORK!**

Where would you take a *T. rex* shopping?

**THE DINO-STORE!**

What do you call a dinosaur that never gives up?

**A TRY-CERATOPS!**

What kind of king would Pencilmate be?

A ROYAL PAIN!

What do you get when you put a crown on a trophy?

A CROWNING ACHIEVEMENT!

Why was King Pencilmate's throne made of pencils?

SO THAT IT WOULD *DRAW* HIS SUBJECTS TO HIM!

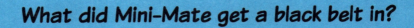

# What did Mini-Mate get a black belt in?

MARTIAL FARTS!

What do you call a pig who takes karate?

PORK CHOPS!

What did Pencilmate drink at karate class?

KARA-TEA!

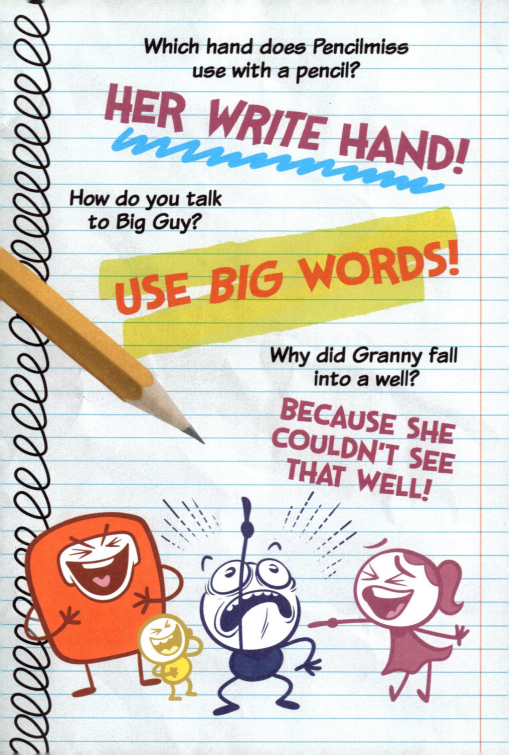

Why did Mini-Mate try to eat his computer?

# HE HEARD IT HAD COOKIES!

Why did Pencilmate's football team yell at the vending machine?

## THEY DIDN'T GET THEIR QUARTER BACK!

**KNOCK-KNOCK.**

Who's there?

**ICY.**

Icy who?

## ICY YOU READING THIS BOOK!

What game does Pencilmate play
during recess?

# HOP-SKETCH!

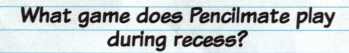

What is Big Guy's
favorite subject?

# MASH-EMATICS!

Why did Pencilmiss bring a
balloon to class?

SHE HEARD
THERE WAS A
POP QUIZ!